PRAISE FOR
PATHWAY TO THE PROMISE

Pathway to the Promise by Pamela Cross is an amazing book with an incredible story about a woman who fell deeply in love with God as a child and her journey of truth through His faithfulness as a guiding force throughout her life. In this book, Pamela takes us on a faith journey and shows the reader how to have and keep the faith of a child while being assured that our God will withhold no good thing from the one who walks uprightly with Him. This book is one of testimony, triumph, and unrelenting commitment and inspiration!

Dr. Hasker Hudgens, Jr.
The Equipping Center
Greenville, South Carolina

A powerful word for desperate times...A determined woman stands on the promises in God's Word as her life ebbs away. The doctors lose hope, but God raises her up. Two decades later, she continues to walk the same pathway of faith, embracing the promises of God.

Linda Youngblood Wright
Friend and Author
Oakland, California

PATHWAY TO THE PROMISE

A Journey of God's Faithfulness

Pamela Cross

JT Publishing House

Pathway to the Promise
Copyright © 2023 by Pamela Cross

Requests to the author for permission should be addressed to:
JT Publishing House, writing@jtpublishinghouse.com

Names: Cross, Pamela.
Title: Pathway/ Pamela Cross.
Description: Spartanburg: JT Publishing House, 2023. | Summary: "As a young attorney, wife and mother, Pamela Cross was diagnosed with lupus, a chronic autoimmune disease that threatened to prematurely end her life. Pathway to the Promise is a memoir of faith, healing, and triumph. Pamela shares her extraordinary story of believing and pursuing God's
powerful promises to obtain total restoration and wellness. She offers practical insight, wisdom and spiritual truth that provides a distinct roadmap for the journey from adversity to triumphant victory. Pathway to the Promise will invigorate your passion for the Covenant Keeping God and build your faith to obtain His precious promises for your life."-- Provided by publisher.

Identifiers: LCCN 2024930621 (print) | ISBN 9781954624207 (paperback) | ISBN 9781954624214 (ebook)
Subjects: BISAC: Religion /Self-Help/ General

LC record available at https://lccn.loc.gov/2024930621

Scriptures taken from the Holy Bible, New International Version®, NIV®. Copyright © 1973, 1978, 1984, 2011 by Biblica, Inc.™ Used by permission of Zondervan. All rights reserved worldwide. www.zondervan.com The "NIV" and "New International Version" are trademarks registered in the United States Patent and Trademark Office by Biblica, Inc.™

Scripture taken from the New King James Version®. Copyright © 1982 by Thomas Nelson. Used by permission. All rights reserved.

Disclaimer: Any internet addresses (websites, blogs, etc.) and telephone numbers in this book are offered as a resource. They are not intended in any way to be or imply an endorsement by JT Publishing House or the author, nor does JT Publishing House vouch for the content of these sites and numbers for the life of this book.

Published by JT Publishing, Spartanburg, South Carolina
www.jtpublishinghouse.com

Printed in the United States of America
10 9 8 7 6 5 4 3 2 1

DEDICATION

I dedicate this book to my loving husband, Eddie Cross. Your love, affection, laughter, adventurous nature, and generous spirit have filled my life with joy and enabled me to become the woman I am today.

You are a devoted father to our children, who love you dearly. You are a mighty man of God who has lived a life of steadfast faith and passionate prayer. I am blessed to be your wife and am glad we are on this life journey together.

TABLE OF CONTENTS

FOREWORD

In the tapestry of life, woven with stories of triumphs and trials, few books resonate as deeply as that of my beloved wife, Pamela's journey of faith. From death's doorsteps to a life of fulfilled promises and victories, the words of this author in the pages of this incredible work you possess will capture your heart.

Over the years, as a spiritual leader speaking all over the world, I've shared countless authentic stories of resilience, faith, and divine interventions using the Word of God as my primary source. Yet, with deep reverence and immense personal connection, I introduce you to the narrative penned by my loving wife in *Pathway to the Promise*.

Situated in Harrisburg, Pennsylvania, our city-wide ministry has been a vessel for personal and professional growth. Literally, hundreds of lives received spiritual empowerment throughout the Capital Region weekly at the Power Lunch. This compelling story of unwavering faith, embodied by my wife, Pamela F. Cross, Esq., strikes a chord that reverberates profoundly within me and, I believe, will resonate with countless souls seeking solace and hope in the arms of God, our loving Father.

Forty years ago, we embarked on the sacred journey of matrimony. We were young, full of dreams and aspirations. Our joys multiplied with the birth of our sons, Jonathan and Brandon. However, as is the nature of life, we were not without our valleys and challenges. Life can be unpredictable, and it presented us with an unexpected storm named Lupus.

My wife, an embodiment of faith from her earliest childhood days and Christ's ardent follower, was suddenly ensnared by this insidious affliction. Nevertheless, amidst this tempest, her enduring spirit of faith in God, fortified by the Word of God, shone brightest. Witnessing my wife, a devoted mother and a brilliant lawyer, confront this monstrous ailment was akin to watching a lighthouse endure relentless waves with her foundation rooted in the bedrock of Christ's promises.

Every day she consumed the scriptures like medicine, by confessing them verbally, feeding her spirit three times a day on God's promises. Like oral medicine, she let the healing power of God's promises course through her veins, rejuvenating her spirit to overcome this attack on her body with stiffness and pain. In the most trying moment, when she was rushed to the hospital, her life hung in the balance; I recalled a defining moment in the hospital's family room with the weight of medical reports pressing down on us. I distinctly heard God proclaim, whispering to my heart and telling me to declare, "She will live and not die, and in not many days, she will rise up and come home with me."

Anchored in Psalm 118:17, "I shall not die, but live, and declare the works of the LORD," I proclaimed this divine assurance to family members and loving friends amid impending death.

While reading this courageous book, you will discover that the supernatural phenomenon that ensued was twofold. Firstly, the incurable ailment vanquished, stumping, yes, baffling the medical fraternity, but we knew the Healer behind the healing. "For I am the LORD who heals you" (Exodus 15:26).

11

All the suffering again affirmed our belief in the Divine Healer and, secondly, the prophecy of our daughter, Candace, a royal decree of our faith and hope during the darkest days of horridness. It was a turning point—a testament to the potency of faith in God's Word. Keep in mind that God wasn't done with His promises. Amidst this tumultuous period, we held onto a vision of our family's future. A daughter. Yes, Candace. We believed, even when circumstances seemed bleak, that our family would soon be graced with the laughter and joy of a baby girl. "Candace" - a promise, a hope, a dream.

As you immerse in every chapter, you will learn how to actualize the principles of faith for your deliverance. Miraculously, as days turned into blessings, we bore witness again to our youngest son, Christian, being added to our family after Candace. The doctors said no more children because they believed the Lupus would return if Pamela became pregnant again, but the God of the impossible created possibilities for us by giving us two more children.

Pamela was restored to health from a sickness deemed beyond cure by medicine. Jeremiah 17:14 affirms, "Heal me, O Lord, and I will be healed; save me, and I will be saved, for you are the one I praise."

Her healing wasn't just a medical anomaly but a divine manifestation. So, why should you immerse yourself in the Pathway to the Promise? Because within its pages lies a living testimony that transcends a personal story. It becomes a universal floodlight for healing for all who put their trust in God. It underscores the way toward the transformative power of steadfast faith. This life-changing book beckons all — the weary, the doubtful, the seekers — to discover the infinite might of God's promises. It's a clarion call to confidence in God, even when the path is obscured, for His Word never returns void.

I ask again, "*Why Pathway to the Promise?*"

Beyond a chronicle of personal triumph, this book is an invitation to journey through valleys and mountaintops, holding steadfastly onto God's promises. It emphasizes that when you digest the Word, believe in His healing, and stand unshaken amidst life's storms, you'll witness the power of God. As Isaiah 53:5 states, "By His wounds we are healed," this book is a real-life story of that truth.

As you read this book, let it not be a story alone but an inspiration. Let it rekindle your faith, hope, love, and the firm belief that our God never fails. This book will be your compass, guiding you through trials and tribulations to the mountain of victory. Let it rejuvenate your trust in His promises. For in His Word, we find comfort, healing, and the undeniable proof of His unwavering love. Jeremiah 30:17 assures, "For I will restore health to you and heal you of your wounds," says the LORD. Dive into these pages and emerge with a rekindled spirit, trusting in the precious promises of God.

With profound love for my wife and fervent hope for all who embark on this illuminating journey, may the Almighty God fill you with His Spirit and bring you to complete health in your body, soul, and spirit.

Pastor Eddie Cross

INTRODUCTION

When I was a child, every summer our family took a one-day trip from our home in Philadelphia to the beach in New Jersey. I loved going to the shore. I loved splashing in the ocean, jumping waves, and having a picnic lunch on the sandy beach. Sand was everywhere at the seashore. It was so plentiful that it was impossible to count.

It reminded me of the story of Abraham that my mother would read to me from the children's Bible when I was a little girl. God promised He would give Abraham offspring as numerous as the sand at the seashore. I remember being immediately captivated by what I heard.

Abraham believed God and God fulfilled His promise.

At a tender age, faith began to rise in me. When I heard that Jesus died for me and

God raised Him from the dead, I believed it and gave my heart to the Lord Jesus Christ while attending Sunday school. I was eager to learn more about the Lord and would read my Bible and attend church faithfully. Just like Romans 10:17 says, "Faith comes by hearing and hearing by the Word of God," so my faith began to grow.

I saw God do marvelous things as my faith in Him and His Word grew in me. My favorite scripture as a teenager was Proverbs 3:5-6, "Trust in the Lord with all your heart and lean not to your own understanding. In all your ways acknowledge Him, and He shall direct your paths."

God granted me the wisdom and skill to achieve academically and directed my steps to attend college and then law school. Along the way, the Lord also gave me my husband, Eddie, a wonderful man of God and my best friend.

As a couple, we put our faith in action, standing on God's promises to provide for us. When Eddie desired a better-paying job, we prayed with believing faith, and God answered our specific request. When I was pregnant with our first child, Jonathan, we found out during my seventh month he was in a breech position–meaning his feet were positioned to come out first during delivery. The doctor began talking about performing a C-section (Cesarean delivery). I wanted a natural delivery and was unwilling to accept the doctor's report.

Activating our faith in this situation, Eddie and I confessed that the fruit of my womb was blessed, and that God would turn him around from his breeched position. Again, God answered our prayers by our faith.

A few weeks before his birth, Jonathan turned around in my womb. I naturally gave birth to Jonathan without using pain medication, and he came out headfirst.

Two years later, I gave birth to our second son, Brandon. With the intervening hand of God and quick action from the doctor, the umbilical cord that was wrapped around Brandon's neck was cut, and he was born alive and healthy. Eddie and I walked by faith, not sight, as we began raising our family and moving into pastoral ministry.

However, in 1995, the genuineness

of my faith was tested like never before. I came under a severe physical attack from the enemy. To make it through this wilderness experience, it would require me to draw upon and rely on the foundation of faith that I developed over the years in my walk with the Lord. I had to trust that the God who gave Abraham seed as numerous as the sand at the seashore was able to perform His faithful promises to me.

Faith rose in me.

I chose to believe the scriptures that promised, "by His stripes, we were healed," even in the face of unbearable pain and seemingly impossible odds. By faith, I called on the Lord to heal me. God did the incredible! He delivered me from the brink of death and restored me to full health.

As you read the story of how God showed His love and faithfulness and fulfilled His promises to me during a season of adversity, I encourage you to have faith, to believe God, take Him at His word, and grab hold of the tangible outcomes God has in store for you, too.

I hope my testimony provides you

with the tools to achieve breakthroughs when you are faced with seemingly impossible challenges in your life.

CHAPTER 1

Candace is Still Coming

Blessed is she who believed, for there will be a fulfillment of those things which were told her from the Lord.
~Luke 1:45

In his calm bedside manner, the attending physician said to me, "Mrs. Cross, you have just come through a major flare-up of lupus. You are fortunate to have survived. I know that you would like to have more children, but I recommend that you not attempt another pregnancy. You have two young sons. Enjoy raising them."

When I heard the doctor's words, I should have been discouraged. I should have been dismayed, but I wasn't. The doctor's words should have dashed all my long-desired hopes of having a daughter. However, his words didn't. In my heart rang other words– words the Lord told me. My heart was full of confidence in the Lord and in His promise to completely make me whole. God had already demonstrated beyond measure to me that He is the "Lord that heals." Just days earlier, I had been in intensive care near death with my lungs 75% percent full of blood, a respirator breathing for me at 100% capacity, and my kidneys failing.

Yet, God, in accordance with the integrity of His Word, showed Himself strong on my behalf by healing me from lupus. Now, I was in a regular hospital room, full of life and breath and recuperating. What the doctor called "survival," I called "victory."

High on the heels of God's favor in my life, I was undaunted by the doctor's prognosis. I remembered Mary, the mother of Jesus, whom the angel had proclaimed was "highly favored" when he announced to her the message from the Lord that she would bear the Son of God. Mary immediately believed. She didn't rely on the limitations of her circumstances but on the greatness of the character of her God.

I, too, was highly favored because God had made the riches of His grace abound toward me in Christ. I, too, believed. As surely as God had delivered me from an untimely death, I firmly believed that He would bring about my complete recovery and enable me to have another child. I rested on the trustworthiness of God and thanked Him that my body was well. Later during prayer, I heard a resounding word in my heart, "Candace is still coming."

I left the hospital a week or so after that particular visit from the doctor, I continued to stand on the promises in God's Word concerning my health, and I believed that God would give me the desires of my heart. When Mary believed, God honored her faith and fulfilled His promise. Nineteen months after my discharge from the hospital, God fulfilled His promise to me as well. Candace Victoria arrived, just as I believed she would.

God has made His promises available not just to me but to all who will believe in Him and His Word.

Questions & Reflections

1. There are a multitude of promises contained in the Bible that God has made for us. Have you been in circumstances where you needed to rely on one of those promises? Describe a situation and the promise you held onto during that time.

2. If you are facing adverse circumstances right now, what scriptures can you use as a foundation to anchor your soul? Make a list of the promises and the scripture verses that you can firmly stand on in faith.

3. How do you arrive at the blessing of a promise fulfilled? What is required on your part? See Luke 1:38.

CHAPTER 2

The Promise of Wholeness

But He was wounded for our transgressions;
He was bruised for our iniquities; The
chastisement for our peace was upon Him;
And by His stripes, we are healed.
~Isaiah 53:5

I woke up on October 19, 1994, refreshed and excited. I was invited to speak at a women's retreat scheduled to begin later in the day. I looked forward to this retreat not only because it would afford me the opportunity to get out of the office for a few days but also, to my delight, it was being held at one of my favorite places–the beach! Based on the schedule, I would spend five days and four nights in a beach house in Dewy Beach, Delaware, with other sisters of faith.

Only one obstacle stood between me and my desire to attend the beach retreat–Jonathan's birthday. If I attended the retreat, I would not be home to celebrate my eldest son's ninth birthday. At first, I wrestled with whether to go to the beach. I felt a little guilty. This would be the first time I would not be home to celebrate with him. How could I not be with him on his special day? After much thought and contemplation, I came up with the perfect solution. I planned a sleepover party for him at a local hotel where he could swim, eat pizza, and have a blast with his friends. With my husband enlisted as the chaperone, and Jonathan thrilled about his upcoming party, I felt relief. Now, I was poised to enjoy my beach retreat guilt-free.

As I arose and packed my belongings to travel to the retreat, my hands felt stiff and achy. I couldn't help but wonder why I was feeling pain. I decided to soak my hands in warm water for a few minutes, and I began to meditate on Isaiah 53. I said to myself, "By His stripes, I am healed." I prayed and asked the Lord to take away the pain, and the pain started to subside.

Later, one of the ladies arrived to pick me up for the ride to the beach. The three-hour drive seemed to pass by quickly as we talked, laughed, and shared our desire to see God move during the retreat. When we got to the beach house, I was amazed. Outside on the front porch, there was a jacuzzi spa. Inside the house was beautiful. There was a fireplace in the sunken family room, a spacious kitchen, and enough bedrooms to accommodate the twenty women who gathered for the event.

I had never been to the beach this late in the season, and although I knew the ocean would be too cold to swim in, I was still excited about being at the seashore. I looked forward to relaxing in the outdoor spa and taking walks along the beach. Most of all, I had great expectations for God to speak to me and the other women as we fellowshipped during our getaway.

During the opening night, everyone played fun, ice-breaker games that allowed us to get to know one another. We also worshiped the Lord together with songs of praise. In the midst of this atmosphere of worship and friendship, Pastor Mary, our conference leader, spoke a message on the glory of God. Afterward, we all sensed the glory of God in our midst, and we spent extensive time in intercessory prayer for one another.

Although it had been a long day, I went to sleep basking in the sweet fellowship of the Holy Spirit and the outpouring of love from sister to sister. I rested well, but when I woke up the next morning, my hands were aching again. A sharp pain pierced through both of my hands, and I wondered why my hands hurt. I thought to myself, "I am too young to have arthritis, and I'm not going to receive it anyway." I refused to allow the pain to stop me from enjoying the blessings that God had in store for me at the retreat, so I got ready for the day.

Pastor Kay, one of the prayer leaders, spoke during the morning session about prayer and the power of God to heal. She shared her testimony of how God healed her daughter after a terrible accident. After her message, she invited those who desired prayer to come forward. I immediately responded to the invitation. For several months I stood on God's Word and believed Him to heal me from a hyperactive thyroid condition, also known as Graves' Disease, and I wanted other believers to agree in prayer with me for my healing. As Pastor Kay and the other sisters laid hands on me and prayed, I believed God would heal my thyroid and my aching hands.

I remained at the retreat for the next several days, blessed by the fellowship and the ministry of the Word. I believed I received my healing from God the moment I prayed and asked Him to heal me. For the next several weeks, however, the achiness in my hands grew worse, and the pain spread up my right arm and shoulder. I felt aches and stiffness in my right arm and shoulder throughout the night and aches in my hands throughout the day. I also began to feel a burning sensation in my back between my shoulder blades that made it difficult to sleep at night.

Nevertheless, each morning during my prayer time, I thanked the Lord for healing me. The pain, however, continued to grow worse and proceeded across my back and down my left shoulder and arm. The joints of my knees began to ache and became stiff. I developed a slight limp as I walked.

I shared with my husband, Eddie, that I was having aches and pain in my body. Eddie thought that maybe I felt pain because I had not resumed my exercise schedule since having foot surgery in August and that my muscles were adjusting from not being

29

used. I agreed with him and began to exercise again. The pain, however, grew worse and continued to expand to my knees and legs.

When I returned home and back to work, my coworkers noticed I had a limp when I walked and asked if my stiffness had anything to do with my recent foot surgery. I told them it had nothing to do with the surgery. I then began to wonder whether I felt stiffness in my knees because I had too aggressively resumed my exercise routine at the gym. I did not know the underlying cause. All I felt was increasing stiffness and pain each day.

In November, I made an appointment with my family doctor, and she ordered a blood test. The test results at the time showed a slight elevation for arthritis. The doctor told me to take Ibuprofen for the pain. Although I took the medication, the symptoms continued to increase, and it became more difficult for me to sleep at night and to walk without pain. One particular night when I felt the burning sensation in my back, Eddie laid hands on me and began to pray. As he prayed, he could see a vision of a black panther with its mouth wide open. The Lord showed him that it was a spirit of jealousy sent against me by the kingdom of darkness and that we needed to engage in spiritual warfare. Eddie began to bind the enemy and prayed for my healing. The burning sensation in my back left my body, and I was able to sleep peacefully that night.

DOUBLE TEAM

The Lord showed Eddie and me that we needed to attack the pain I experienced on the spiritual, physical, and emotional levels. Spiritually, prayer and the confession of the Word of God became paramount. Eddie anointed me with oil and prayed the prayer of faith in accordance with James 5:14-16.

Each day Eddie and I prayed, read the Word, and stood on God's promises. Physically, I began to soak in Epsom salt each evening, and Eddie rubbed my body down with Bengay and other ointments to help soothe the pain. Emotionally, I needed to lighten up my days with laughter. The scriptures link laughter to healing. Proverbs 17:22 declares that "A merry heart does good, like medicine."

I was confident that the Lord was my

healer, and I was poised to endure until I was free of the illness. Yet, as I went about my daily activities, I did not smile because of the intense pain I felt. I came to realize that the expression on my face did not mirror the confidence in God that I felt on the inside. I began to read funny stories and watch comedies to make myself laugh and smile. Having fun with my husband and sons made my heart merry, too. Such joy and laughter became medicine to my soul.

While I confessed that I was healed, the pain and stiffness grew worse. One morning during my devotions with the Lord, He showed me there was a spirit of infirmity trying to bind me and hold me in captivity.

The arthritis that prevented me from moving freely in the physical realm was an indication of what the devil was trying to do in the spiritual realm. Prompted in my spirit, I read Luke 13:10-16, where Jesus sees a woman in the synagogue, on the Sabbath, who is bent over and could not raise herself up because she had a spirit of infirmity for eighteen years. Jesus called her over to Him and said, "Woman, you are loosed from your infirmity."

Jesus then laid hands on her, and immediately she stood straight and glorified God (Luke 13:13). However, the ruler of the synagogue was indignant and chastised the crowd for seeking healing on the Sabbath. Jesus responded to the hypocrite by stating, "Ought not his woman, being a daughter of Abraham, whom Satan has bound–think of it–eighteen years, be loosed from this bond on the Sabbath?" (Luke 13:16).

Here this woman was a daughter of Abraham, a daughter of the covenant promises of God, who had been robbed for eighteen years of her rightful inheritance of physical wholeness and well-being because of a spirit of infirmity and bondage from the devil. The devil had no right to bind this woman.

God's covenant with Abraham included healing from diseases, sicknesses, and infirmities. Jesus knew and understood the covenant promises, spoke them over this woman, and broke the chains that bound her. Jesus is the Word of God; He is the Truth. He spoke the truth about this woman and exposed the lie and deception of the devil. The devil had to release her because he had illegally bound her. Jesus, the Truth, was present,

33

and the devil was subject to Him. Jesus was also Lord of the Sabbath, and healing was available to this woman and anyone else, even on the most sacred day.

I began to stand on God's promise that I was a daughter of Abraham and that I was loosed from my infirmities, too. According to Galatians 3:6-7, God accounted me as one of the multitudes of descendants of Abraham, as one of the innumerable grains of sand at the seashore, because I was full of faith and believed in God just like Abraham. With confidence, I began confessing aloud, "I am loosed from my infirmities, I am whole, and I am not bound."

The Lord also showed me that a spirit of death was attacking me. I bound the spirit of death and declared that it had no authority over me.

Although the pain and stiffness grew worse, I continued to confess my healing. Each night I continued to soak, and Eddie continued to rub my body with ointment. On my next visit to the doctor, she prescribed a higher dosage of Ibuprofen for the pain. By Thanksgiving, I could barely move without pain.

At the age of 33, I was walking around like an older woman. I had difficulty going up and down the stairs and getting in and out of the car. If I didn't take the medicine, the pain became unbearable. I hated taking medicine, and I didn't want to depend on it, but the pain and stiffness persisted.

My seven-year-old son, Brandon, laid hands on me and prayed in faith, proclaiming, "He lays hands on the sick, and they do recover" (Mark 16:18). I decided to fast for three days starting on the evening of December 12. Midway through this period of fasting, I visited my doctor, and she ordered another blood test. Based on the test results, I was diagnosed with lupus.

In my spirit, I refused to receive the doctor's negative report. When I shared the diagnosis with my husband, I didn't even want to say the word "lupus" out of my mouth because I rejected it from the outset. I did not understand what it was, and I was not going to receive it. I was determined to stand on the promise of complete wholeness.

Questions & Reflections

1. Two powerful scriptures related to healing are found in Isaiah 53:5 and 1 Peter 2:24. What can you learn from these passages, and how can you apply them when seeking healing for yourself or someone else?

2. The prayer of faith is essential to obtaining healing. According to James 5:14-15, what happens when we incorporate the prayers of the body of Christ when we face sickness and adversity? How can our prayer of faith be effective in the life of another person?

3. Christ is our Redeemer. Christ redeemed us from the curse of the law. He became a curse for us so that we could be blessed (see Galatians 3:10-14). Read Deuteronomy 28 and thank God for granting blessings and redeeming us from curses.

4. Reflect on that notion that we worship a faithful and loving Heavenly Father who has provided a wonderful promise in 1 Thessalonians 5:23-24, "Now may the God of peace Himself sanctify you completely; and may your whole spirit, soul, and body be preserved blameless at the coming of our Lord Jesus Christ. He who calls you is faithful, who also will do it." As you meditate on His promise, may your trust in His faithfulness increase and give you the confidence to receive the complete wholeness that He intends for you.

PATHWAY TO THE PROMISE

CHAPTER 3

The Promise of Forgiveness

And whenever you stand praying, if you have anything against anyone, forgive him, that your Father in heaven may also forgive you your trespasses.
~Mark 11:25

Eddie and I had been married for eleven years when I received the diagnosis of lupus. Over that period of time, as with any marriage, we had experienced our ups and downs, our disappointments and hurts.

As an introvert, I tended to be quiet and reserved and would hold my feelings inside. Even when things bothered me, I would hold things in and thought it was enough to resolve any conflict. Unknowingly, I was building a volcano of unresolved issues by stuffing away the hurt and pain. I didn't realize the emotional and even physical harm I was doing to myself. After I shared the diagnosis with Eddie, he did some research and found out, among other things, that lupus is linked to bitterness and a tendency to hold things in emotionally. I knew that certain illnesses had a spiritual or emotional root cause to them.

This newfound information on lupus was an eye-opener. It was key to further tapping into my healing. Because I desperately wanted to be healed, I did not want any bitterness or lack of forgiveness to hinder me.

One of the most endearing gifts my husband gave me during this season of physical affliction was his complete transparency. Eddie afforded me the opportunity to ask him about anything that bothered me or about anything that I had bottled up over the years. He recognized the benefits of forgiveness, and he willingly dialogued with me to set in motion this essential key to my recovery.

That conversation took place on a Friday night after we conducted a marriage seminar at Victory Christian Center in Philadelphia. After teaching about the marriage covenant, we went to my parent's home to spend the night. Instead of sleeping, we spent the entire night in bed talking and sharing, confessing and repenting, forgiving, and clearing the air between us.

James 5:16 states, "Confess your faults one to another and pray for one another that you may be healed."

We actively applied this principle, and our relationship was made whole and stronger. Forgiveness brought us closer together in agreement. After all, oneness is what the marriage covenant is really all about. We were now free to tackle the enemy together on one accord. Not to leave any stone unturned, I also began to think about whether there were other people in my life that I had not forgiven. I began to visualize various individuals, and I forgave and released them in my heart. I felt free and knew that I was not holding anything against anyone.

That Sunday, we visited Eddie's dad, who is a pastor in Wilmington, Delaware, and shared the diagnosis with him. He stood in agreement in prayer with us for my total healing.

When we arrived back home in Harrisburg later that evening, Eddie and I also shared my diagnosis with another pastor and his wife, and they agreed in prayer for my healing from lupus. This precious couple loaned me a cassette tape containing a message by Norvel Hayes entitled *Framing Our World with Our Words*. This tape became a part of the arsenal of weapons I used against the enemy.

Armed with the Word, prayer, forgiveness, and laughter, Eddie and I added communion to our strategy of spiritual warfare against the devil. Each night for the next week, we took communion to remember that the Lord shed his blood for my redemption and that His body was broken for my healing.

Questions & Reflections

1. Those who have been forgiven much love much (Luke 7:47). Does your love life with the Lord reflect how much He has forgiven you? Pause and adore Him if you are thankful that He has forgiven you.

2. Jesus said that the commandments could be summed up into two, namely, to love the Lord God with all your heart, soul, and mind; and love your neighbor as yourself (Luke 10:27). Have you loved yourself enough to forgive yourself for past mistakes and failures? How does our confession of our faults to another trusted believer facilitate our own healing? See James 5:16.

3. Are there people in your life who you need to forgive? Whether you realize it or not, unforgiveness holds you captive to the persons who hurt or offended you. There is power in forgiveness. Forgiveness releases you from bondage to the offense and the

offenders. Forgive the ones who hurt you and set yourself free. It may not be easy, but you can do it through the power of the Holy Spirit. By faith, decide as an act of your will and not based on your feelings to forgive. Make a mental paradigm shift. Replace the negative images of the offenders in your mind with images of how Jesus sees them. Jesus sees them as forgiven by His shed blood, and you should see them that way, also.

Now, pray for their well-being by praying that they have an encounter with the Lord to receive salvation or be brought into a more intimate relationship with Him if they are already born again. When you think about them, pray blessings over them and not curses. Line your prayers and your mouth up with the will of God for their lives. Be empowered with forgiveness.

CHAPTER 4

The Promise of a New Deal

And He took the bread, gave thanks and broke it, and gave it to them, saying, "This is My body which is given for you; do this in remembrance of Me." Likewise, He also took the cup after supper, saying, "This cup is the new covenant in My blood, which is shed for you."
~Luke 22:19-20

I am absolutely convinced of the mighty power of the blood of Jesus. Jesus' life, as with all life, is in the blood. When Jesus died on the cross, He shed His blood and gave His life for you and me.

Jesus' blood speaks volumes.

The blood of Jesus is eternal and

testifies before the throne of the Father that I am forgiven and cleansed from all my sins. Jesus' blood testifies that I am free from the bondage of the kingdom of darkness. The blood of Jesus testifies that I am healed of all my sicknesses and diseases.

The blood of Jesus, the spotless Lamb of God, speaks better things than the blood of bulls and goats. The blood of Jesus ushered in the new covenant. I have a new agreement with the Father that I am saved, healed, and delivered through the blood of Jesus.

Knowing these truths and appropriating them in my life gave me strength each day, even as I faced much physical pain. The Bible says that "by the mouth of two or three witnesses, every word may be established" (Matthew 18:16).

Jesus, who is the Word of God, is a witness. The blood of Jesus is a witness. The Word and the blood are formidable witnesses in the face of the devil, the accuser of the brethren.

I made the decision to bear witness to the same testimony of Jesus and His blood in order to establish the truth of His word in my body. During these beginning stages of my sickness and not knowing how long it would take for my healing to manifest, I boldly said in faith, "I am an overcomer by the blood of the Lamb and the word of my testimony" (Revelations 12:11).

Questions & Reflections

1. There is power in the blood of Jesus. Write down some ways you have personally experienced the power of the blood of Jesus in your life.

2. We can testify to the things we have seen, heard, or experienced. What is your personal testimony as a believer in Jesus Christ? Write down a brief testimony of your salvation, healing, or deliverance.

3. Read Luke 22:14-20 and meditate on the significance of the body and blood of the Lord Jesus. Participate in communion at home or at church with renewed revelation.

CHAPTER 5

The Promise of the Spoken Word

And since we have the same spirit of faith, according to what is written, "I believed and therefore I spoke," we also believe and therefore speak.
~2 Corinthians 4:13

Eddie and I were blessed with two wonderful sons, Jonathan and Brandon, and we were tenderly and happily nurturing and raising them. We loved our boys dearly and wanted to have more children. One of the bright spots in the midst of my illness was finding out before Christmas that I was pregnant. For me, this was the greatest Christmas gift ever. We were all overjoyed with the good news and looked forward to a new baby, hopefully a girl.

On Christmas day, one of the gifts I received was a Walkman cassette player. That evening as I went to bed, I played the cassette tape of Norvel Hayes' message. I listened to that tape over and over for the next several days. On the tape, Reverend Hayes shared the testimony of a woman who had lupus and believed God for her healing and began to give daily confessions that lupus would not kill her. Within a year, she was completely healed of lupus. This tape encouraged me and helped to build my faith. I began to confess that lupus had no authority over me, that lupus could not kill me, and that Jesus was Lord over my body.

From Christmas to the end of December, I continued to boldly confess that I was healed and delivered. I took the Word like medicine. I wrote out my own personalized confession of faith and verbally declared it throughout the day.

MY PERSONALIZED GOOD FAITH CONFESSION:

I confess Jesus is my Healer.

Jesus' healing power is flowing through my body right now.

Jesus' healing power that is flowing through my body is destroying and dissolving lupus, arthritis, Graves' disease, and all manner of sicknesses and diseases.

Lupus, I'm talking to you; you cannot kill me. Lupus, I command you, in Jesus' name to come out of my body right now. Be removed from my body, in Jesus' name.

Arthritis, I'm talking to you; you cannot kill me. Arthritis, I command you in Jesus' name to be removed from my body.

Graves' disease, I'm talking to you. Be removed from my body in Jesus' name. Graves' disease, you cannot kill me.

Jesus is my Healer. Jesus is healing me now!

The number of my days, He will fulfill.

I say I am healed, delivered, set free, and victorious in Jesus' name.

Thank you, Father, that your Word says I can have whatever I say. Therefore, I say I am healed, delivered, and set free.

I submit (worship) to God, and the devil flees from me.

Satan, your works have been destroyed. For this very purpose, Jesus was manifested to destroy the works of the devil.

I resist you, Satan, and you must flee from me.

Pain, I'm talking to you, and I command you to come out of my body now in Jesus' name.

Stiffness, I command you to come out of my body now in Jesus' name.

Lupus, arthritis, Graves' disease, and all your symptoms come out of my body now in Jesus' name.

I shall live and not die.

I found that confessing the Word of God in faith was vital for my recovery. It was important for me to renew my mind in the Word of God. I looked at the Word and not at the physical symptoms that were manifesting in my body. I chose the truth of God's Word over the reality of the pain I experienced in the natural realm.

Yes, it was a real pain, and I felt it, but I refused to focus on the physical symptoms. I chose to walk by faith and not by sight (2 Corinthians 5:7). Walking by faith required me to focus and rely on God's spiritual laws, which are superior to and supersede all natural laws.

The symptoms of lupus (natural law) contradicted the truth of the Word of God (spiritual law). Accordingly, I made a conscious effort to disregard what I saw and felt in the natural, and I lined my mouth up in agreement with the Word of God through my good faith confession. I found scriptures to stand on and claimed them as my inheritance and possession in the Kingdom of God. I spoke forth the intended results of my healing and not the symptoms. I visualized myself as healed and whole.

I prayed the scriptures, and I brought God's Word before Him, giving voice to the scriptures in my prayers. I refused to fear. I believed in accordance with the scriptures that the law of the Spirit of life in Christ Jesus set me free from the law of sin and death (Romans 8:2).

In the final days of 1994, I received a rhema word from the Lord from the passage of scripture found in Romans 8:11. The Lord said to me, "The same Spirit that raised Jesus from the dead dwells in [you] and gives life to [your] mortal body."

Jesus lived in me, and His Spirit lived in me; therefore, I took God at His word and believed that His indwelling Spirit would give renewed life, strength, and vigor to my physical body.

A preacher once said, "Faith is not seeing. Faith is thanking God for something before you ever see it, and Jesus will let you see it."

Along with my confession of faith, every day, I thanked the Lord for healing me. With thanksgiving flowing out of my heart and mouth, I believed that Jesus would let me see the manifestation of healing in my body in due season.

Questions & Reflections

1. To confess means to say the same thing; to acknowledge. When I confess sin, I acknowledge my wrongdoings. When I make a good faith confession, I acknowledge the truth of what God has said about me in His Word, and I say the same thing in agreement. Here are a few confessions of faith that you can make about yourself based on God's Word:

I am a child of God. (Romans 8:16; 1 John 3:2)

I am an heir of God and a joint heir with Christ. (Romans 8:17)

I am blessed. (Ephesians 1:3; Galatians 3:9)

I am saved. (Romans 10:9-10)

I am healed. (Psalm 103:3; 1 Peter 2:24)

I am delivered from the power of darkness and translated into the Kingdom of the Son of His love. (Colossians 1:13)

I am forgiven. (Psalm 103:3; Colossians 1:14)

I am the head and not the tail; I am above only and not beneath. (Deuteronomy 28:13)

I am a new creation. (2 Corinthians 5:17)

I shall not die but live and declare the works of the Lord. (Psalm 118:17)

2. There are over 7000 promises of God in the Bible that can meet your every need. What promise can you lay hold of and begin to confess in faith to address your need today?

CHAPTER 6

The Promise of Freedom

And you shall consecrate the fiftieth year and proclaim liberty throughout all the land to all its inhabitants. It shall be a Jubilee for you, and each of you shall return to his possession, and each of you shall return to his family.
~Leviticus 25:10

With the dawning of 1995, a new year was upon us. Eddie and I declared that this was our year of Jubilee, our year of joy, our year of release from bondage and debt. We proclaimed, "This is 1995, and we will not be denied!"

I began to feel less pain and stiffness in my joints and was able to move about more freely. I was not only physically pregnant but also full of great expectations of seeing the manifestation of my complete healing from lupus.

In January, I had my first visit with Dr. Rubin, the rheumatologist my primary care physician referred to me. He shared a wealth of information about systemic lupus erythematosus (SLE), the type of lupus afflicting me. I learned that lupus is an autoimmune disease whereby the body's immune system attacks normal healthy tissues. The inflammation and joint stiffness I experienced were symptoms associated with SLE. Other symptoms of SLE include swelling and damage to joints, skin, kidneys, blood, the heart, lungs, and other connective tissues.

Dr. Rubin attributed the lessening of my symptoms to my pregnancy. Since the lupus symptoms were being masked by the pregnancy and not currently manifesting, he told me to contact him after I delivered the baby. He cautioned me, however, that after giving birth, it was highly likely that I could experience a lupus flare-up with a return of the joint pain, stiffness, and inflammation of the connective tissues in my body.

I was so happy that I would not have

to deal with the pain and stiffness of lupus during the next eight months that I was not intimidated by his remarks. With lupus at bay, I would be able to enjoy my pregnancy and focus on delivering a healthy baby. I seized the opportunity to anchor myself in the Word of God as I stood in faith against the disease.

I soon came to realize that the devil's onslaught was about to intensify. Within a week of my doctor's visit, I began spotting blood. I contacted my obstetrician, who sent me to have an ultrasound. The results of the ultrasound indicated that I was either in the initial stages of a miscarriage or I was going to have twins. Eddie and I were optimistic that we would be having twins.

A couple of days later, on Super Bowl Sunday, our family was invited to a party to watch the game. As we got ready to go, I went to the bathroom, and to my dismay, I saw heavy bleeding and a large clot pass from my body. I mustered the strength needed at the moment and went to the party, but I knew I had a miscarriage. The next day, blood tests confirmed what I already knew. My joy turned into sorrow. I had never experienced a miscarriage before. I leaned on Eddie and drew strength from him. Although he felt the same disappointment, he comforted and encouraged me. He reminded me that just as one of our friends had delivered a baby after having a prior miscarriage, God would do the same for us because of His faithfulness to keep His promises.

We comforted one another by saying that our twins were in heaven and that one day we would see them there. I also called my friend, who shared from her heart about her own experience with a miscarriage. I realized that it was okay to grieve the loss of our babies and was greatly encouraged by her story.

Jonathan and Brandon were also sad and disappointed when we told them about the miscarriage. We comforted them and told them that I was young, and God would still give us a new baby in His time.

After the miscarriage, the masked lupus symptoms began creeping back on the scene. Just as Dr. Rubin had predicted, the joint pain and stiffness returned to my body. On a trip to see my parents in Philadelphia, my mother gave me a copy of Charles Capp's booklet, *God's Creative Power for Healing*. She saw the extreme pain that I was in, and she prayed for me. Throughout February and into the month of March, I continued to take God's Word as medicine. I boldly declared, "The Word is healing my body. The Word is made flesh in my body."

Due to the increase in pain, Dr. Fischer, my family physician, prescribed a higher dosage of Ibuprofen (800 mg) and started me on Prednisone which I began taking on March 22. On the same day, I noticed a purple, raspberry-colored one-inch patch on my right index finger. I made a note to inform Dr. Rubin about this at my upcoming appointment scheduled for Monday, March 27.

In the middle of the night on March 23, 1995, the Lord awakened me and prompted me to read Mark 5:21-43. In the midst of this passage, I read, "Do not be afraid. Only believe." This was a personal rhema word from the Lord to me, that is, a word spoken directly to my heart.

I went back to sleep and arose again at 6:00 AM to pray, as was my habit, and I received another rhema word. This time the Lord prompted me to read Luke 4:18-21. It states:

The Spirit of the Lord is upon Me,
Because He has anointed Me
To preach the gospel to the poor;
He has sent Me to heal the
brokehearted,

To proclaim liberty to the captives
And recovery of sight to the blind,
To set at liberty those who are
oppressed; To proclaim the acceptable
year of the Lord.

Then He closed the book, gave it back
to the attendant, and sat down. And
the eyes of all who were in the
synagogue were fixed on Him. And
He began to say to them, "Today this
Scripture is fulfilled in your hearing."

I had read this passage many times before. I understood Jesus was anointed to heal the brokenhearted, proclaim the gospel to the poor, restore sight to the blind, set captives free, and proclaim the acceptable year of the Lord. I understood the phrase "the acceptable year of the Lord" as a reference to the Year of Jubilee and liberty for those bound by debt (see Leviticus 25).

I understood Jesus was our Jubilee

and had come to set us free from our debt of sin as well as our financial debts. As I was reading this passage this particular morning, the Lord very clearly said to me, "You know, that's not just financial. That's whatever the debt may be, whatever the chain or captivity. Whether it is a sickness, whatever type of bondage, whether it is financial, spiritual, or physical bondage, I have come this day to release you. The anointing is here to release you from bondage."

Lupus is symbolic of bondage. It is a very binding type of disease that immobilizes you with stiffness. You want to move, or you want to pick something up, and you can't. Lupus symbolized to me the bondage that the adversary wanted to put me in. I refused to receive that bondage. The voice of the Lord speaking to me from Luke 4 only intensified my resolve to stand fast in the liberty to which Christ had made me free (Galatians 6:1). Although I was in extreme pain physically, I was strengthened in my spirit.

Before I left for work that day, I said to my husband, "You know we are proclaiming this year as our year of Jubilee. This is 1995, and we will not be denied. We want to go forth and proclaim that message.

Well, the Lord is showing us that He is going to deliver us from some things. He is going to bring us out of captivity so that as we go and proclaim this to others, we can come not only from what the Word of God says but also from our own experience that God has brought a tremendous victory."

The next day Eddie went on a business trip out of town. He was away the entire weekend. On Saturday morning, Jonathan and Brandon got up and watched their favorite cartoons as they normally did and then completed their chores. I woke up with an urgency to accomplish three things that day. I wanted to work on our tax returns, go grocery shopping and attend an open house of new homes being built in our township.

Armed with my agenda in mind, I went to the mall to buy a calculator so I could complete our tax returns. I then went to the open house, sat down with the realtor, and designed the customized home of my dreams. We rented a townhouse since moving to Harrisburg, and it was our desire to buy our own home or have one built.

At the open house, I selected the lot location for the home and the type of flooring and appliances I wanted inside. I told the realtor that when my husband returned from his trip, we would put down a deposit. As I talked with the realtor, I was in much pain and hot with a fever, but I pressed my way because this was a step of faith on our journey toward homeownership. I then went to the grocery store to buy items to make our dinner. After getting home and preparing dinner, I had no strength left to tackle our tax returns.

By the end of the day, I noticed red raspberry marks on my right thigh. During the night, the low-grade fever persisted. Unwilling to succumb to symptoms, I went to church to worship the Lord in the midst of my weakness. After church, I could only lay on the couch for the remainder of the day. I was so exhausted and in pain that I could not muster the strength to laugh along with Jonathan and Brandon as they watched "Pete and Pete," one of their favorite television shows on the Nickelodeon channel.

I managed to go to work on Monday, and that afternoon I attended my appointment with Dr. Rubin. I described my symptoms and showed him the purple raspberry marks that had appeared on both my finger and thigh. Since he only had a copy of the results of a former blood test that was not showing much lupus activity, he advised me to continue to take Prednisone as prescribed by Dr. Fischer. He said once he received my updated blood test results, he would contact me and provide further directions as appropriate.

In the face of all these symptoms, I kept in mind the promise that Jesus is my Jubilee.

Questions & Reflections

1. What does Jesus is my Jubilee mean to you? Meditate on Luke 4:18-21.

2. In what areas of your life do you feel bound? You can be released from your bondages by taking advantage of your inheritance as a child of God. Jesus' purpose in coming was to destroy the works of the devil (1 John 3:8), and He accomplished that through his death, burial, and resurrection and won our freedom. As a believer, you have authority over the devil. Memorize Luke 10:19 and exercise your authority over the devil through the name of Jesus.

3. Today, proclaim and make a good faith confession that you are released from every form of bondage and debt. Profess, "Jesus has set me free" (John 8:36).

PATHWAY TO THE PROMISE

CHAPTER 7

The Promise of Light

The Lord is my light and my salvation; whom shall I fear? The Lord is the strength of my life; of whom shall I be afraid?
Psalm 27:1

A major flare up of lupus was brewing in my body. The full impact of the disease was confronting me head on. I recall vividly what was happening to me during the onslaught of this medical crisis. I share the events as they unfolded before me during those critical days.

Tuesday, March 28, 1995

I went to work after meditating on various healing promises and confessing healing scriptures as medicine. I used Charles

Capp's book on *God's Creative Power for Healing* and read Kenneth and Gloria Copeland's *Healing Promises.*

While at work, I started coughing. My cough continued all morning. Around 11:00 AM, I began to cough up blood. I was not alarmed because I thought I had burst a blood vessel in my throat because of how hard I kept coughing.

At noon, I left my office to walk over to the Power Lunch, a Tuesday bible study and lunch that my husband and I held for downtown workers. As I walked the three blocks to the Pine Street Presbyterian Church, where we gathered for the Power Lunch, I noticed I was short of breath. When I arrived at the church, I immediately went to the restroom and coughed up blood for five minutes or so. By the time I came out of the restroom, Eddie was already at the podium, opening the session with prayer, so I did not have a chance to talk to him. I grabbed a bowl of soup and sat down.

Eddie spoke on the topic of the "Keys to the Kingdom." As soon as he finished the message, I asked my friend, Shelly, who had driven to the church, if I could ride with her back to my office. I did not talk to Eddie because I felt so tired, and Shelly was ready to go. I immediately left with her, along with several others who were getting a ride.

As soon as I arrived back at my office, I called Dr. Fischer. Unfortunately, she was out of the office for lunch. After I hung up, Dr. Rubin called me to tell me he had received my blood tests from Dr. Fischer's office, and it showed that my kidneys were not functioning properly.

When Dr. Rubin finished talking, I told him I was coughing up blood. He told me to call Dr. Fischer. "She's currently taking her lunch break. I just called the office moments ago," I shared.

"I will have her paged," he said.

I called Dr. Fischer again at 2:30 PM, as instructed by Dr. Rubin. She told me to go to one of the local medical imaging facilities for an X-ray.

I immediately left my office. As I headed toward the parking garage to my car, I ran into the pastor who loaned me the Norval Hayes' cassette tape. I told him where I was going and gave him a brief overview of what was occurring. He asked if I needed a ride, and I assured him that I did not but thanked him for the offer.

Once I reached my car, I asked the Lord for strength to make it to the X-ray facility.

Although weak and coughing frequently, I made it to the facility. I know that it was the Holy Spirit who enabled me to drive there safely.

After my X-ray was taken, Dr. Fischer spoke to me over the phone about the results. She informed me that my lungs were filled with blood. She told me to go home and have my husband take me to the hospital. I drove home and called Eddie.

A short while later, Eddie arrived and he got Jonathan, Brandon, and me into the car. We dropped the boys off at the home of one of the members of our church and proceeded to Polyclinic Medical Center, where I was admitted as an inpatient.

Later that evening, Dr. Rubin came in and shared with us the three procedures that could be done collectively to get the symptoms under control. The initial step would be to place me on a higher dosage of Prednisone. The next step would be to undergo a blood plasmapheresis to filter my blood. The last step would involve taking a chemotherapy medication called Cytoxan intravenously. Once he described the procedures to me, he recommended that I pursue this course of action. He also stated that he would schedule a kidney biopsy for me.

Yearning for the symptoms to abate, I was fine with everything the doctor said. God created everything and He could use all available resources to aid me. I decided in my heart to cooperate with the process laid out before me trusting in God's providence. Eddie prayed with me and left for the evening.

Wednesday, March 29, 1995

My body is weak. I am still coughing up blood, but I am hopeful.

Eddie came to my room mid-morning. Delighted to see him, I smiled and greeted him affectionately. Eddie shared that he had informed family and friends that I was in the hospital, and they were praying for me. As we talked about the road ahead, I took Eddie's hand, looked him in the eyes and said, "Things look dark now, but I know that the Lord is bringing us through and that this is the dark just before the light at the end of the tunnel."

Eddie squeezed my hands and nodded in agreement.

"Remember the first theological discussion we had when we met and began dating back in 1979 about long life? Well, if there are no other promises to stand on, I know that God has promised me a long life because I have honored my mother and father," I declared.

Although not a typical healing scripture, Ephesians 6:1-3 (KJV) states, "Children obey your parents in the Lord: for this is right. Honour thy father and mother; which is the first commandment with promise; that it may be well with thee, and thou mayest live long on the earth."

Eddie and I continued our conversation never once uttering the words death or dying. We trusted the Lord to bring about full healing and recovery. When Eddie shared his thoughts that I should follow the doctor's directions to take the chemotherapy medication, I totally agreed with him. As we further discussed the things we needed to take care of concerning the boys and our finances, I committed everything over to Eddie completely trusting his wisdom and discretion.

In the afternoon, my mom and my sister, Dottie, arrived from Philadelphia. I was overjoyed. Their presence refreshed my spirit. We talked and shared stories until it was time for dinner. Eddie took them to our home for the evening.

Later, I had a long phone conversation with my brother, Thomas, who lives in Atlanta. He introduced me to Vivian, a woman at his church who had lupus. With a deep understanding of what I was experiencing, Vivian shared her amazing testimony of God's goodness in her life. Thomas prayed for me and said his congregation would be praying for me as well.

Before I went to sleep, I received a call from our spiritual mentors, Bishop Gideon A. Thompson, and his wife, Pastor Yvonne Thompson. They encouraged me and prayed for my healing.

Thursday, March 30, 1995

This morning, I moved to the intensive care unit to have the kidney biopsy and blood plasmapheresis.

Around 11:00 AM, Eddie arrived with my mom and Dottie. Shortly thereafter he left to go to the Power Lunch. Mom and Dottie kept me company for an hour or so then had to leave to travel back to Philly.

Once I was alone, it seemed as if the clock slowly ticked away. Feeling thirsty, all I could think about was having a sip of cranberry juice, but because of the upcoming biopsy, I could not eat or drink anything.

The biopsy finally started at 2:30 PM. The procedure went well, but immediately after, I still could not drink because the medical staff was ready to perform the blood plasmapheresis.

"How long will the procedure last?" I asked.

"Three hours," the nurse said.

I persevered through those hours, waiting until I could drink again. Although it seemed like forever, the procedure was over, and I was finally able to have cranberry juice and rest a little. However, throughout the day, I continued to cough up blood.

In the evening, the medical staff gave me an oxygen mask instead of the smaller nose tube I had been using since my arrival at the hospital. Eddie came to visit along with three brothers in the Lord. After watching my favorite television program, ER, a TV drama about doctors working in a hospital emergency room, I went to sleep.

During the night, the nurse woke me up to take my temperature and check my vital signs. The respiratory technician prepared a new oxygen mask for me. I looked at the nurse and noted how efficient she was. Then, I coughed a big cough and passed out. That is the last thing I remember.

VALLEY OF THE SHADOW OF DEATH

From that point on, I was totally in the Lord's hands. I was not conscious for the next six days. When I came to, I learned from

Eddie the details of what had happened.

On the night I passed out, Eddie received a call from the hospital, and the doctor's report was not good. The doctor told him I was experiencing kidney failure and that my lungs were seventy-five percent filled with blood, so the medical team had placed me on a respirator.

Although the respirator was operating at one hundred percent capacity, I was still not breathing effectively. The doctor did not know how long I would live and told Eddie he should come in right away along with Jonathan and Brandon because they might not see me again.

Eddie chose not to bring our sons in to see me. He came Friday morning alone and refused to fear. Despite what he saw and heard, Eddie stood firm in faith and on God's Word.

The people of God near and far prayed for me. Churches in the city had all-night prayer meetings. Bishop Thompson flew in from Boston and prayed. A brother in the Lord stayed in my room all night praying, singing, and reading scriptures. Prayer

THE PROMISE OF LIGHT

continued throughout Saturday.

Eddie told me that so many friends and family members showed up at the hospital that the visitor's room overflowed.

The Lord impressed in Eddie's heart, and told him to declare, "She will live and not die, and in not many days, she will rise up and come home with me."

Eddie received the word with gladness.

On the next day, Sunday, there was a complete turnaround in my condition, and I began to breathe more on my own.

JESUS' SLAM DUNK

Although the enemy had performed a full-court press against me to steal, kill, and destroy me, the Lord Jesus Christ did a slam dunk on the devil by healing my body and delivering me from the brink of death. What the enemy intended for evil, the Lord used as an opportunity to show Himself strong on my behalf and to bring glory to His name.

When I became fully alert on April 5, 1995, I could not believe that I had missed several days of my life. I did not recall being anywhere but asleep. During that period, the Lord watched over me. He watched over my body, my soul, and my spirit. He kept me and brought me out, healed and whole, answering my prayers and the prayers of the saints.

Over the next several days at the hospital, I began regaining strength in my body. I went from being incubated on a respirator, to having it removed and fully breathing on my own. My white blood count increased, and my kidneys functioned properly.

The doctors and nurses were amazed at my recovery and progress. I gave glory to the Lord for healing me and boldly told the doctors and hospital staff about the miracle God performed in my body. One doctor on staff did not want to acknowledge the hand of God but would only say that it was because of the love of my husband that I had come through. In further testimony of the miracle, I said to him that it was the love of God that made me whole and the love of my husband.

Questions and Reflections

1. According to Ephesians 6:1-3, what is the secret to living a long life?

2. The power of love is formidable. What does love have to do with long life? Reflect on Psalm 91:14-16.

3. What words of wisdom do you learn from Proverbs 4:20-23 regarding health and life?

4. Read Acts 10:38. What was Jesus anointed to do? How do you benefit from Jesus fulfilling His purpose?

CHAPTER 8

The Promise of the Overflow

*You will show me the path of life; In Your
presence is fullness of joy; at Your right hand
are pleasures forevermore.*
~Psalm 16:11

My physical body was recovering.
My soul was filled with gratitude thanking
and praising the Lord. I was also thankful for
the doctors and nurses who helped me and
for all the people who prayed for me. My
spirit was overflowing with immense love
and exuberant joy. I also felt a heightened
sensitivity to the voice and presence of God.

One night while still in the hospital,
I had several dreams when I went to sleep.
In the first dream, I saw myself opening
a door and being in a dark room with one

chair illuminated by a spotlight. I remember thinking, if I am going anywhere, it's up!

Then I saw my body in a lying position, rising to the sky in the darkness. I was being raised up to Jesus. I could not see His face, but He stretched out His hand and touched my rib cage area, and my chest illuminated. Then, I began to float back to earth. As I came down, it was dark, and imps and demonic forces began raising their heads. I said in my heart, "I don't have to fear because I have my weapons. I can pray in tongues. I can bind the enemy."

I saw myself floating in the clouds with the wind of the Spirit. I then came over a ridge and was on a city street. I began to look at the people's faces and saw that they looked in despair. I began to say to myself that they needed to hear about Jesus. I heard someone say, "Tell Teddy," and then I saw a train arrive. I awoke from my dream.

That last dream really resonated with me. My dad, Theodore Fritz, had worked for the railroad for 40 years until he retired. Although my mom called him Fritz, his coworkers called him Ted. Seeing the train and hearing the name Teddy, I believed the dream was about my father and that the Lord called me to tell my dad about Jesus' saving grace again.

Some years prior, I shared with him about God's plan of salvation and how he could invite Jesus into his life. To my surprise, he said he could not be forgiven. I didn't have a comeback at that time, and the conversation ended. However, I continued to pray for my dad, as I have for other family members, standing on the promise in Acts 16:31 that "my household would be saved." I didn't realize the prophetic nature of my dream at the time. Within a matter of days, God set the stage for a divine appointment.

That unexpected appointment happened on the Saturday before Easter. I had been in the hospital for nearly three weeks. I was longing to go home to spend Resurrection Sunday with my family. I didn't think that my desire would come to pass that quiet day at the hospital. To my surprise, Dr. Rubin came to my room and informed me that he would discharge me in just a few hours. This was wonderful news.

My hope was becoming a reality. I could not be discharged right away, however, because Eddie had taken the boys to Phila-delphia to shop for their Easter outfits. When I called Eddie to tell him the good news, he had just arrived in Philly, and it would take him a while to get back to Harrisburg.

I decided to relax and wait patiently for his return. Soon after getting off the phone, I had a visitor. To my amazement, it was my dad. He had taken the train up from Philly and had managed to take a city bus from the train station to the hospital.

I was so glad to see him. I immediately recalled the dream and felt an urgency to witness to him. This time, I was armed with the right ammunition, the love of God. I told my dad he did not have to concern himself with the Lord not forgiving him because the Lord had already forgiven him. There was no sin that he had committed that Jesus had not already forgiven him for by His death on the cross and resurrection from the dead.

This time it stuck, and my dad was ready to receive the Lord. I led him in a prayer of salvation, and he gave his heart to Christ. I saw this time together alone with him in the quiet hospital room as an orchestrated plan by the Lord. Seeing my dad saved that day was worth the journey of sickness and healing I endured.

Glory to God!

Eddie arrived at the hospital late Saturday afternoon, and I was discharged to go home.

The following day, Easter Sunday, I was home celebrating the holiday with my husband and two sons. That Resurrection Sunday held special meaning for me. I rejoiced in the God of my salvation because I was alive and well. Jesus sacrificed His life on the cross for me so I would be saved. He took 39 stripes on His back and was pierced so I would be healed. He wore a crown of thorns so that I would be delivered from the curse of sin and death. As He was raised from the grave, I was raised to new life in Christ Jesus, spiritually and physically.

BRANDON'S SONG

I was so happy to be back home with my husband and two boys. I knew that it must have been difficult for Jonathan and Brandon to be without their mom for so long. I was curious about how they managed to cope so I asked my sons what helped them make it through this difficult time while I was away in the hospital. I thought they were going to recite a favorite Bible verse or a song they learned in church. To my amazement, Brandon said he would sing himself the song, "These Are the Days of the Year," that he learned in elementary school.

For years later I wondered why he sang that song to carry him through. Over time, I started to see his song was a prophetic song. As Brandon sang, "January, February, March and April, May, and June, and July; August, September, October, November, December; these are the months of the year, yes, these are the months of the year," he was prophetically singing that I would live to see the days, months, and years to come.

MY LOVE POEM

After I was home, I continued to pray, praise and worship God. I never considered myself to be a poet, but one day a creative expression of God's profound love for me flowed as a poem.

THE PROMISE OF THE OVERFLOW

God loves me with an everlasting love that knows no bounds.

God has poured forth His love upon me today immeasurably.

I receive His love.

Questions & Reflections

Poetic Utterances

1. Take a moment to pen a love poem to adore the Lord. Let your tongue be the pen of a ready writer (Psalm 45:1).

Prophetic Utterances

2. To prophesy is to tell forth and to foretell the Word of God. You prophesy every day when you speak God's Word over your life or the lives of others. Pause, listen to the inner voice of the Lord, and begin to speak forth His Word over your life, the lives of your family, and others. Believe to see the goodness of the Lord in the land of the living (Psalm 27:13).

CHAPTER 9

The Promise of Fruitfulness

*I am the vine; you are the branches. He who
abides in Me, and I in him, bears much fruit;
for without Me you can do nothing.*
~John 15:5

THROUGH FAITH AND PATIENCE

We live in a microwave, high-speed
internet, instant gratification generation.
We could aptly be called Generation Now
because we want what we desire instantly–
right now.

Have we lost the discipline of waiting?

During my physical affliction, I
constantly stood on God's Word that He was
my healer and my deliverer. Through prayer,

worship, and meditation on the Word of God daily, I developed an intimate relationship with the Lord. I knew His name, Jehovah Rapha, the Lord Who Heals. I knew His character and trusted in His impeccable integrity to make me whole again.

My heart trusted in the Lord, although my body was in pain. My body longed for a speedy recovery to health. One day the Lord prompted in my spirit that we often like things to happen quickly, even automatically. We want to see the results right then and there because of the promise of the Lord. The Lord, however, took me down a progressive path to my healing. On this journey, He showed me that it is "through faith and patience that we inherit the promises" (Hebrews 6:12).

As far as God was concerned, I was already healed. I was healed the moment I put my trust in Him to heal me from lupus. I was healed back when Jesus was beaten, when He wore the crown of thorns upon His head, taking on every curse on my behalf, and when He shed His blood for me on the cross at Calvary. The timing of the manifestation did not negate the fact that the Lord was my healer.

There was a part that I needed to play. I needed to participate in the miracle by using the spiritual fruit made available to me as a spirit-filled believer. It was my responsibility to "imitate those who through faith and patience inherit the promises" (Hebrews 6:12).

Faith and patience are part of the fruit of the Spirit, and all the fruit work together. Galatians 5:22-23 lists all the elements of the fruit of the Spirit: love, joy, peace, longsuffering (patience), kindness, goodness, faithfulness (faith), gentleness, and self-control.

I activated the spiritual fruit of faith the moment I believed, but what would help me to arrive at the destiny of my hope and expectation?

I learned that I needed to partner the spiritual fruit of patience with my faith in order to obtain the full manifestation of healing in my body.

Faith says, "I am healed."

Patience says, "I am confident in the character of God. Therefore, I can wait (rest) in Him with the assurance of the intended outcome."

Faith is the action of believing. Patience is the action of persevering.

Patience enabled me to persevere through the long months between when I believed and when I received my miracle. The time gap tested the genuineness of my faith (1 Peter 1:7).

Romans 5:3-4 instructs us that "tribulation produces perseverance (patience) and perseverance produces character and character, hope."

The physical attack on my body brought on by the devil was a season of enormous tribulation. I fought for my life. I could not give up or quit. I had to fight the good fight of faith and endure to the end. My faith was fired up, and I was determined to win. The devil threw his fiery missiles to see if my faith was genuine.

Did I really believe God and what He said in His word?

Would I hold on or give up?

Would I be discouraged by the length of time of the battle?

I used the shield of faith to quench the fiery darts (bitter words, doubts, and fears) of the enemy. I also called on patience to step in and assist my faith. When my flesh got weary, I rested in the name and character of the Lord and let patience have its work.

I humbled myself and waited. I waited just like a little girl waits while her mom braids her hair, with the expectation of a beautiful hairdo. My expectation was complete healing; therefore, I visualized myself as wonderfully healed. This vision of a marvelous outcome helped me to endure.

The scripture passage in James 5:10-11 states, "My brethren, take the prophets, who spoke in the name of the Lord, as an example of suffering and patience. Indeed, we count them blessed who endure. You have heard of the perseverance of Job and seen the end intended by the Lord–that the Lord is very compassionate and merciful."

The Lord was very compassionate and merciful to me, too. As I persevered and patiently waited on Him during the testing of my faith, the Lord walked with me and brought me out of the fire into the place of my hope and expectation–total healing.

COUNT IT ALL JOY

Faith's partner is patience. Patience's partner is joy. James 1:2-4 says, "My brethren, count it all joy when you fall into various trials, knowing that the testing of your faith produces patience. But let patience have its work, that you may be perfect and complete, lacking nothing."

I found that the secret to perseverance is going through with joy. Joy was absolutely necessary. Without joy, my patience would have been hindered. Joy altered my viewpoint. The spiritual fruit of joy helped me to rejoice in the Lord instead of focusing on the adverse conditions surrounding me.

The joy of the Lord was my strength (Nehemiah 8:10) for the journey as I worshiped Him in the midst of my trial and circumstances. Jesus was anointed with the oil of gladness above his companions (Hebrews 1:9). Because of the joy of seeing us saved, healed, and delivered, He endured the cross and overcame the enemy. That same anointing of joy was mine as a part of the body of Christ, and I tapped into it. By praising and worshiping, I entered the presence of God where there is fullness of joy and at His right-hand pleasures forevermore (Psalm 16:11).

BOUNTIFUL FRUIT

The testing of our faith is the fertile ground in which the fruit of the Spirit can grow. Sometimes we have one part of the fruit developed more than another. When my faith was tested, I needed to rely on all aspects of the fruit of the Spirit working together–love, joy, peace, patience, and gentleness. The testing of my faith enabled my patience to grow. Operating in joy allowed patience to have its complete work in me.

Joy produced gentleness (Philippians 4:4-5). My love even increased during this season because I realized how much God loved me. God made me more than a conqueror because of His love, and nothing, not even death or life, can separate me from the love of God.

"For I am persuaded that neither death nor life, nor angels nor principalities nor powers, nor things present nor things to come, nor height nor depth, nor any other created thing, shall be able to separate us from the love of God which is in Christ Jesus our Lord" (Romans 8:38-39).

As I waited on the Lord, He gave me peace in my heart. Philippians 4:6-7 assured me that the peace of God would guard my heart and mind. As I pressed on, I saw more and more fruit getting bigger and bigger in my life. The Lord delivered me, and I gained a great harvest of spiritual fruit and blessings.

GENUINE FAITH

As I read the First Epistle of Peter, the Holy Spirit gave me an understanding of the purpose, the process, and the produce (fruitfulness) of my fiery trial. What I initially thought took too long was actually just a little while in the scope of eternity.

I learned that the fire was not there to destroy me but to prove to the Refiner that my faith was more precious than gold. This genuine faith displayed the praise, honor, and glory of Jesus Christ to the world and to the devil. The result of faithfully enduring gave me unspeakable joy for my healing, deliverance, and salvation.

The Apostle Peter summed it up best with his words: In this, you greatly rejoice, though now for a little while, if need be, you have been grieved by various trials, that the genuineness of your faith, being much more precious than gold that perishes, though it is tested by fire, may be found to praise, honor, and glory at the revelation of Jesus Christ, whom having not seen you love. Though now you do not see Him, yet believing, you rejoice with joy inexpressible (unspeakable) and full of glory, receiving the end of your faith–the salvation of your souls (1 Peter 1:6-9).

I had genuine faith.

Questions & Reflections

1. If you have lived long enough, you have faced a wilderness experience or a fiery trial. Perhaps you have asked the Lord for an explanation for why you were going through those trying times. Have you considered that God sees something deeper in you than you may see on the surface?

A refiner's fire gets the impurities out of the gold so that it is unadulterated and proven to be of great worth. You are of great worth to God, your Father. His goal is to get to the hidden treasure inside of you. God sees your faith as more precious than gold, and He delights to show off the genuineness of your faith to the world, to demonic forces, and to all creation. Arm yourself with the principles found in 1 Peter 1:6-9 and make your Abba Father proud the next time you are in the fire.

2. Why is it important to have the fruit of the Spirit operating in your life? How do faith, patience, and joy interrelate with one another as you grow in the Spirit? Study Galatians 5: 22-23, Romans 5:3-4, and James 1: 2-4.

3. Notice the phrase "oil of gladness" in Hebrews 1:9. Oil is a lubricant, and it can soothe. Oil can also be infused with a pleasant fragrance. Oil is a symbol of the Holy Spirit. Being filled or anointed with the Holy Spirit includes receiving joy. Walk in the anointing of joy with the fragrance of the Spirit.

In Isaiah 61:3 we are told to put on the garment of praise for the spirit of heaviness. Our rejoicing is in the Lord as we focus on Him, not on the circumstances. We delight in the goodness of our God, knowing that He will never leave us nor forsake us. Amid a trial, in what tangible ways can you tap into the spirit of joy to carry you through your adversity?

CHAPTER 10

The Promise of Victory

For whatever is born of God overcomes the world. And this is the victory that has overcome the world—our faith.
~I John 5:4

In Chapter 1, I shared with you the glorious ending at the beginning. I wanted to whet your appetite to follow along the pathway with me to the fulfillment of the promise of God in my life. What God has done for me, He can certainly do for you.

Jesus is always victorious! As His Bride and a member of His Body, you are victorious, too.

Faith is the victory that overcomes every adversity, attack, trial, or fiery dart that the devil or the world hurls at us. God made a promise to the believer that our faith will enable us to live victoriously.

When our daughter was born in December 1996, it was only fitting that we named her Candace Victoria because her birth was a confirmation of my total healing and victory in Christ Jesus. To add a cherry on top of His marvelous work, two years and four days after Candace's arrival, Christian Kenan was born. God provided a double blessing to wonderfully confirm my healing and deliverance from lupus. He gave us Candace and Christian as lasting, living evidence of His power to heal.

With our victories, we must also be vigilant. Our adversary, the devil, goes about as a roaring lion seeking whom he may devour (1 Peter 5:8). He will attempt to steal, kill and destroy because that is his nature. Every day, as believers, we must resist the devil staying steadfast in faith (1 Peter 5:9). If we submit to God and resist the devil, God promises that the devil will flee from us (James 4:7). It is a daily vigilance, and we must not let down our guard and become complacent.

Four months after Christian was born,

he developed a severely high fever and was diagnosed with bacterial meningitis. Eddie and I found ourselves back in another battle with the enemy. Faced with this challenge, we again engaged in spiritual warfare. We took up the shield of faith and put on the whole armor of God (Ephesians 6:10-18). We prayed and interceded for our son and asked for others to stand in prayer with us. Christian was healed, and another victory was won.

Hallelujah! Praise the Lord! I have overcome the devil, and his attack of sickness and affliction on my family and me, by the blood of the Lamb and the word of my testimony (Revelations 12:11). I have absolutely no lupus disease in my body. I have been healed by the Lord.

Questions & Reflections

1. Luke 1:45 is one of my favorite scriptures. I like to personalize it and place my name in the scripture when believing God for one of His promises. You can do the same. Commit this passage to memory.

2. Both 1 John 5:4 and Revelations 12:11 give us insight into how we overcome adversity and demonic attacks. In your own words, how does a child of God overcome and live victoriously?

3. Can anything separate you from God's love? What makes you more than a conqueror? Read Romans 8:31-39.

AUTHOR'S NOTE

As I approach nearly 30 years since the Lord healed me, I can boldly say that my healing still stands. After a recent blood test, my doctor reaffirmed what I already knew to be true that there is no lupus in my body. This is undeniable and unshakable proof of God's faithfulness to His promises.

When we follow the pathway to God's promises we will be transformed spiritually, physically, emotionally, financially and in every area of our life. We can have a new beginning.

I have become a brand-new person. I have new tools to take on challenges and overcome.

My faith is stronger.

I am blessed.

I am blessed with peace and a sound mind. I am blessed with a loving and flourishing family. I am blessed with a fruitful and productive life. I am ready to embark on the new adventures God has in store for me.

I invite you to press forward to your breakthrough by standing on the promises God has made available to you and experience the blessings. If you are facing any sickness, disease, or adversity, read and meditate on the Healing Scriptures provided on the following pages. Believe what the scriptures say, proclaim them out of your mouth and apply them to your life.

I also have provided a Healing Prayer at the end of this book. Adapt it to your specific illness or as you pray for others. Use it to strengthen your faith. Pray with bold confidence. Thank God in advance expecting the incredible demonstration of His faithfulness.

Finally, go for victory and follow the pathway to the promise.

HEALING SCRIPTURES

Genesis 18:14a

Exodus 15:26

Exodus 23:25-26

Psalm 103:1-5

Proverbs 3:7-8

Proverbs 4:20-22

Proverbs 17:22

Isaiah 53:5

Isaiah 58:8, 11

Matthew 8:17

Matthew 9:18-22

Mark 5:21-34

Mark 11:22-24

Mark 16:17-18

Luke 8:41-48

Acts 10:38

Romans 8:11

James 5:14-15

1 Peter 2:24

1 Peter 5:7

2 Peter 1:2-4

HEALING PRAYER

Lord Jesus, I thank you that you have come that I might have life and have it abundantly.

I thank you for an abundant life. Thank you for redeeming me from sin, sickness, and disease. I thank you for redeeming me from the curse of the law. Therefore, I boldly declare that sin, sickness, and disease have no dominion over me.

Lord, you are my Creator and my Healer. Thank you for making my body operate in perfect wholeness because you have fearfully and wonderfully made me. I command every illness to depart from my body in the name of Jesus.

Jesus, you bore my sins in your own body on the tree (cross), and by your stripes, I am healed. I am already healed, and I say so based on the authority of your Word.

My kidneys and lungs are healed.

My joints are elastic and function as God created them to function. I command pain and discomfort to leave my body in Jesus' name.

Lupus, arthritis, and joint pain have no dominion over me. I am free from lupus.

My blood, circulatory and respiratory organs are well and are working in accordance with God's perfect design.

My body is the temple of the Holy Spirit. God who raised Jesus from the dead gives life to my mortal body through His Spirit who dwells in me.

The Spirit and the Word infuse healing virtue and restoration throughout my body.

I do not and will not worry, for I give you, Lord, all my worries and fears.

I cast them on you because you care for me.

Bless the Lord, oh my soul and all that is within me.

Bless the Lord, oh my soul, and forget not His benefits. I bless Him who forgives all my iniquities, heals all my diseases, redeems my life from destruction, and crowns me with loving kindness and tender mercies (Psalm 103:1-4).

I thank you, Lord, for healing me. I believe by faith that I am healed. My faith is in your Word and in your promises. My faith is not in how I feel. The number of my days I will fulfill in health because the blood of Jesus covers me. Thank you, Father, for healing me.

I am healed. I am blessed. You are Jehovah Rapha, the Lord, my Healer.

In Jesus' name, Amen.

ACKNOWLEDGEMENTS

I give thanks first and foremost to my Lord and Savior Jesus Christ, who is the Promise Maker and Promise Keeper. All the promises of God in Christ Jesus are yes and Amen.

I thank my amazing husband, Eddie, who has inspired and encouraged me to stretch beyond my comfort zone and to pursue all my dreams.

I thank my awesome children, Jonathan, Brandon, Candace and Christian, who have given me the joy of motherhood and the blessings of seeing each of them live a life of significance and destiny in Christ.

In loving memory, I thank my mother, Mildred Fritz, who planted the seed of the Word of God in me when I was a child.

I also thank Gina Worthy for providing her professional counsel and guidance to help me jump start my writing process.

Finally, I thank Jossalyn Wilson and JT Publishing House for their excellence and professionalism in publishing this book and making my dream a reality.

AUTHOR'S BIO

Pamela Cross has been involved in pastoral ministry, along with her husband, Eddie Cross. She currently serves as part of the ministry team at Living Spring Harrisburg Church.

Pamela is a life-long seeker of knowledge. She is a dedicated student of the Bible, an engaging teacher of the Word of God and an admired mentor transforming the lives of people of all ages.

With a passion for the nations, she travels globally to share the gospel and to build the body of Christ. Through the anointing of the Holy Spirit, Pamela brings a message of healing, deliverance, and restoration for those who are thirsty for the Fountain of Living Water.

Pamela is a graduate of Cornell University and the University of Pennsylvania

Law School. She is an accomplished attorney who has completed a distinguished 31-year career with the Commonwealth of Pennsylvania in the Governor's Office of General Counsel. She was elected and serves as Commissioner in Susquehanna Township, Dauphin County.

Pamela has been married to Eddie for 40 years and they have four adult children and one grandchild.

Connect with Pastor Pam online at:
www.pamcross.com

www.ingramcontent.com/pod-product-compliance
Lightning Source LLC
Chambersburg PA
CBHW051537120626
46551CB00012B/1256